CAN YOU TELL ME
WHAT TIME THE MIRACLES HAPPEN?

GERARD EATON

Can you tell me
what time
the miracles happen?

ST PAULS

Acknowledgements: My thanks to Fr Patrick Sayles, of the Columban Fathers, for permission to reprint the article by Fr Patrick O'Connor entitled "I met a miracle", the story of Jack Traynor. Thanks to the editor of the *Lourdes Magazine* for permission to reproduce photographs 5 and 6; Casa Editrice Bonachi 4 and 7; Bruner & C. 2; Editions P. Chambon 9; A. Giovannini (© Edizioni San Paolo srl) 1; A. Tarzia (© Edizioni San Paolo srl) 10; R. Risitano 11.

Cover design by Mary Lou Winters fsp; photo by Cipriano Caneva © Edizioni San Paolo srl

ST PAULS
Middlegreen, Slough SL3 6BT, United Kingdom
Moyglare Road, Maynooth, Co. Kildare, Ireland

© Gerard Eaton 1995

ISBN 085439 501 6

Set by TuKan, High Wycombe
Printed by The Guernsey Press Co. Ltd, Guernsey, C.I.

ST PAULS is an activity of the priests and brothers of the Society of St Paul who proclaim the Gospel through the media of social communication

Contents

For Imelda,
a loving wife and devoted mother

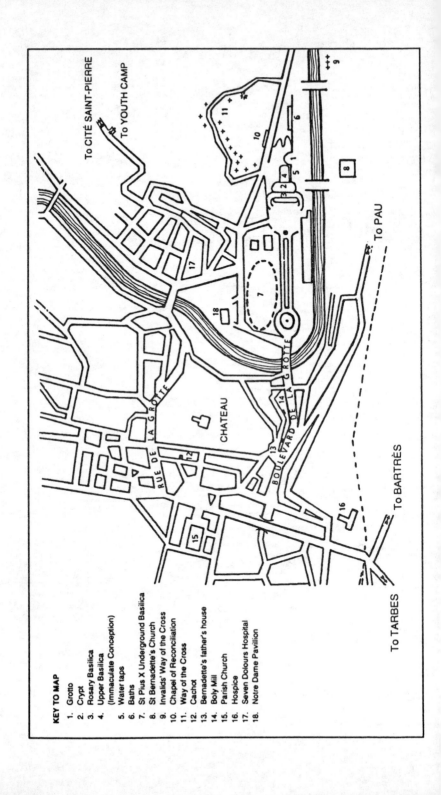

KEY TO MAP

1. Grotto
2. Crypt
3. Rosary Basilica
4. Upper Basilica
   (Immaculate Conception)
5. Water taps
6. Baths
7. St Pius X Underground Basilica
8. St Bernadette's Church
9. Invalids' Way of the Cross
10. Chapel of Reconciliation
11. Way of the Cross
12. Cachot
13. Bernadette's father's house
14. Boly Mill
15. Parish Church
16. Hospice
17. Seven Dolours Hospital
18. Notre Dame Pavilion

To CITÉ SAINT-PIERRE

To YOUTH CAMP

To PAU

To BARTRÈS

To TARBES

CHATEAU

RUE DE LA GROTTE

BOULEVARD DE LA GROTTE

Lourdes today remains one of the most frequented of Catholic shrines. More than four million visitors and pilgrims come each year to the Grotto of Massabielle, where the Virgin Mary appeared to Bernadette Soubirous eighteen times, in the year 1858. The Archives of the Medical Office go back to 1878. Thousands of cures have been recorded, yet only sixty three proclaimed miraculous. Visitors occasionally arrive at the "Domaine" and ask "What time do the miracles take place?" The answer is that miracles are taking place all the time, the vast majority spiritual, rather than physical.

St Bernadette said "The Lady was always smiling at her." She continues to smile perhaps laugh, at the antics pilgrims get up to each week. This collection of stories and experiences might bring a smile to your face, or a tear to your eye. The writer hopes you may feel encouraged to visit this rather extra – ordinary place. A place once described as a "Little bit of Heaven upon Earth".

Introduction

On the 11th February 1858, Bernadette Soubirous, the fourteen year old daughter of a poor miller, went with her sister Marie-Antoinette, and Jeanne Abadie to gather firewood from the woods by the river Gave, at a place now called the Grotto of Massabielle. A beautiful young lady appeared to Bernadette. She was clothed in white, a white veil over her shoulders and arms reaching almost to the hem of her white dress. She had a yellow rose on each bare foot. The sash of her dress was blue, and she had a rosary on her right arm. Bernadette took out her own rosary, and imitating the girl she made an indescribably beautiful sign of the Cross, which was to be admired by everyone who saw her cross herself.

There followed eighteen apparitions during which the Lady made known her instructions to Bernadette. On the 18th February she said to Bernadette "Will you do me the favour of coming here for fourteen days." On the 21st February the Lady said to Bernadette "Penance, penance, pray for sinners". On the 25th February she said "Go and drink at the spring and wash yourself in it". Bernadette scraped the ground with her fingers and soon a muddy coloured trickle of water appeared, this soon developed into a torrent.

On the 2nd March the Lady said to Bernadette "Go tell the priests that I wish a chapel to be built, and processions to come here". However the priests, in particular the Parish Priest, Fr Peyremale wanted to know where the money was coming from to build this chapel, and who was this "beautiful Lady", who wanted processions.

Thus it was on the 25th March 1858, the Lady joined her hands and uttered the words "I am the Immaculate Conception". So that she would not forget these words (which she did not comprehend), Bernadette repeated them over and over to herself as she ran to the presbytery. The Parish Priest heard Bernadette blurt out "I am the Immaculate Conception."

Bernadette never said that cures would take place in Lourdes. However Lourdes is renowned throughout the world as the town of miracles. Physical cures are few compared to the spiritual cures. Grace which transforms lives, is the hallmark of this extraordinary place. It is a place of grace because it is a place of prayer, of penance and of suffering. The sick have pride of place, and perhaps the greatest contradiction that is plain to witness, is the happiness that permeates this place, where so much suffering is concentrated. People on pilgrimage in Lourdes find a peace and joy that reaches to their innermost being. Their souls become alive. In Lourdes they are touched by Heaven.

Lourdes is a sign to mankind of the existence of something quite beyond the humdrum world known to the natural sciences. It's physical miracles display the Lordship of God over the world, and they underline yet again, the love God has for man, especially those who have asked his mother to intercede on their behalf.

These signs of God's power arouse our attention to the fundamental search for truth, for happiness, for peace. They are not arbitrary displays of God's omnipotence, but deliberate interventions in this world, which have but one purpose, to draw mankind to God, and make him the focus of each individual life.

The French Solution

In the Summer of 1976 a twenty year old University student arrived in Lourdes with one of the English Pilgrimages. Her arrival was a monumental mistake caused by bad communication among over zealous Christians. Elizabeth was a paraplegic and had been confined to a wheel chair since the age of eight. She had dark hair, large eyes but she never smiled. She was an atheist. Her mother had been told that handicapped people could have an inexpensive holiday in the Pyrenees, at a place called Lourdes. Medical care and supervision were free. The travel arrangements were duly made, and the young lady arrived at Dover to take the ferry which connected with a night train. At Dover she was upset to see so many sick people, and in particular the number of priests and nuns.

The train eventually arrived in Lourdes. It began to dawn on Elizabeth that someone had made a colossal blunder. Far from going on holiday, she was at the centre of a religious pilgrimage. She decided to take positive action. As soon as she arrived at the hospital, she asked to speak to the Pilgrimage Director. The Director together with one of the chaplains were found. Elizabeth then asked if she could return to England without delay. She explained to the chaplain that she did not believe in God, and felt most unhappy at having been brought to a Catholic place of Pilgrimage. The chaplain suggested that perhaps because she was in Lourdes, this could be a sign from

God that he wanted her to believe. Elizabeth replied that she had studied religion and she did not believe in the existence of God, she continued "I don't believe in Jesus, or Mary or all the superstitious mumbo jumbo that surrounded the Catholic faith." She added she wanted nothing to do with the pilgrimage, Lourdes or priests. She wanted to go home.

A conference was held. The Travel Agents could not get a seat on a plane. There was no-one available to accompany her back by train. She would have to stay. The situation was explained to her. Elizabeth reluctantly accepted the position, but on certain conditions. First, that she was not pestered by do-gooders, or by priests, trying to convert her. Second, that she was not to be asked to go to any of the processions, or religious ceremonies. Thirdly, that she might be afforded the opportunity of visiting the Pyrenees, the local places of scenic interest, and be taken into the town. She had brought plenty of books and would undertake some study.

Three days passed, Elizabeth visited cafes, went on coach trips, wrote cards and letters and studied. Her requests were strictly adhered to by the priests, the pilgrimage organisers, and all who were in daily contact with her. By now her opinions were well known. As far as religion was concerned the subject was taboo.

At about this time of year, there are over 50,000 pilgrims, who journey to Lourdes from every part of the world. Lourdes is a place of prayer, and a place where miracles do occur. There are the physical miracles but the majority are miracles of grace where a person's life often takes a dramatic new direction.

However, in the case of Elizabeth, a non-believer was this to be the exception? Any form of conversion was improbable. First she was an avowed atheist, second no-one was allowed to talk to her on religious matters, thirdly it was forbidden to take her to any religious ceremony. She abhorred religion, she regarded it as superstitious. God did not exist and all the trappings, surrounding Mary, Lourdes, the rosary, exemplified the very worst of religious gullibility. From every viewpoint her conversion was not just improbable, it was impossible. Nevertheless, Elizabeth was in a very remarkable place. Someone had special plans for this girl. What occurred was quite extraordinary in it's simplicity.

On the fourth day, a Wednesday, the entire pilgrimage attended the International Mass, concelebrated in the vast underground basilica dedicated to St Pius X. About 25,000 pilgrims entered the basilica for the 9 o'clock Mass – that is – with the exception of Elizabeth. All the sick and handicapped pilgrims left the hospital at 8.15 am for the basilica. About 118 sick, some on stretchers, others in wheelchairs. By 9.00 am the hospital was quiet, totally still, except in the front courtyard, alone, sitting in a wheelchair, reading, was Elizabeth.

The scene was set and this is what happened. At 9.30 am. Phillipe Garade a 24 year old Frenchman had gone to the Astoria Hotel to take a sick pilgrim to the International Mass. He found to his annoyance that someone had already taken the pilgrim. The Hotel is next to the hospital, so the Frenchman decided to visit the hospital in the hope of being of some assistance to a handicapped pilgrim. Phillipe could not speak a word of English. To his amazement and consternation the first person he saw was a girl in a wheelchair. He soon found out she was English. The air went blue with French expletives. "They have left

this sick handicapped pilgrim behind." Phillipe realised it was too late to take this paralysed girl to the
International Mass, so instead he decided the best
place for such an attractive "Anglaise" was the Grotto.
Smiling and nodding his head, he began to push
Elizabeth. For her part, Elizabeth was quite charmed
by this handsome young Frenchman, although communication was difficult. However, it was approaching 10.00 am and coffee in one of the cafes seemed
appropriate. Phillipe seemed oblivious to the cafes as
they passed them by, he headed towards the entrance
to the Domain. At this point, Elizabeth became genu-
inely alarmed, her consternation turned to anger and
she started to shout at the Frenchman. "Take me back
to the hospital." Phillipe not understanding a word
marched steadily on. They entered the Domaine.

For the first time Elizabeth saw the magnificent
statue of Our Lady. They crossed the Esplanade in
front of the Rosary Basilica, and approached the Grotto
where Our Lady had appeared 18 times to Bernadette
Soubirous. Let Elizabeth continue. "I saw a large rock
with a niche and in this niche was a statue of a young
girl. There were about 100 or more people kneeling,
and all were praying. The young Frenchman stopped
me in front of the Grotto. He knelt down and took out
a rosary. I looked up and looked around and for the
first time in my life I had the extraordinary sensation
of total peace. Phillipe then took me to the waters of
Lourdes. I drank some water and he splashed some
on my head, arms and legs. We then started our
journey back to the hospital."

By this time, the entire pilgrimage, the sick, the
doctors, nurses, pilgrims, priests and bishops had
returned to the hospital. Panic ensued. Where was
Elizabeth? Search parties were sent around the cafes

and restaurants. The Bishop was informed. At about 11.30 am Phillipe entered the hospital pushing Elizabeth. They were immediately surrounded by officials of the pilgrimage. In quality French studied with colourful adjectives, Phillipe told the assembled priests and officials what he thought of their total disorganisation. Anglo-French relations at that point sank to an all time low. Phillipe departed. Elizabeth was taken back to her ward. Then it happened – she asked to see the chaplain. "Father would you teach me to say the Rosary?" The priest dumbfounded could scarcely believe his ears. He knelt down beside her chair and started her instruction.

Elizabeth went to every Mass and all the Services, and she asked to be taken to the Grotto every day. The most amazing physical change in the girl was in her face. It was radiant, she never ceased to smile. Elizabeth was received into the Catholic Church four months later, and subsequently both her parents became Catholics.

20,000 Dollar Signature

In the mid sixties an American lady died and in her Will she bequeathed $20,000 to Our Lady of Lourdes. The New York lawyers executing the Will had never heard of this titled Lady, let alone Lourdes. Nevertheless, it was decided to locate the Lady, an investigation was initiated.

After considerable geographic research, it was established that the only Lourdes in the world, was a small town at the foot of the Pyrenees in southern France. Accordingly a letter was sent to the Mayor of Lourdes. In their communication, the lawyers explained they were trying to track down "The Lady of Lourdes", who was a recipient under a Will. They asked the Mayor to let them have her full name and address, if alive, alternatively her next of kin. In addition, the letter continued, they would be most grateful if the enclosed documents could be passed onto "the Lady", or her French notaries. The Mayor was completely baffled by the letter and the documents. He sent the package to the legal department for interpretation.

The French Notary in his memorandum to the Mayor stated the following: –

A Bequest of $20,000 was available subject to the following:

1. The full name of Our Lady of Lourdes
2. Her permanent address
3. Her next of kin
4. Her signature on all the documents duly witnessed by a notary.

As soon as the Mayor had finished reading this extraordinary letter, he decided to pass the problem to the Hospitalite of Our Lady of Lourdes. The package and letters were sent to the President of the Hospitalite. Having digested it's contents, the President sent for Peter Crane (R.I.P.). Peter, an Englishman, was a member of the Council, and had lived in Lourdes for many years, fortunately he was blessed with a wry sense of humour.

He faced the President and said "The decision is quite simple, comply with the legal requirements."

Full Name	Mary, Mother of God
Permanent Address	Heaven
Next of kin	Jesus Christ
Signature	–

Peter continued, "as far as the signature is concerned, you could place the documents in the Grotto, after all," he continued, tongue in cheek, "since the money will be used for Catholic purposes, perhaps she will sign?"

The President who could not understand English humour, decided Peter was being facetious. Then Peter said, "Perhaps the Bishop could sign in place of Our Lady?"

Eventually all the documents, duly signed by the Bishop, witnessed by a notary, were returned to the United States, together with a letter, and a booklet giving the details of the Shrine of Lourdes.

The $20,000 was not sent. Two months later, two Americans presented themselves at the Mayor's office and handed over a cheque for $20,000 and another cheque for $5,000, a gift from the New York firm. The lawyers stayed in Lourdes for several days, and since that time come regularly to Lourdes on pilgrimage.

In-Flight Conversion

Jacques was 52 years old, a senior executive in a Paris based export company. He and his wife lived in a Paris apartment during the winter, and in the summer they moved to their country house. Jacques' wife was a devout Catholic, he was not. Although their married relationship was reasonably secure, Marie's religious fervour began to build up a barrier between them, in fact it had the effect of making Jacques anti-religious. Jacques had stopped attending Mass and the sacraments for over twelve years.

Every June Marie went on a pilgrimage to Lourdes. Every year she tried to persuade Jacques to accompany her. Every year Jacques refused point blank. However, in 1987 Jacques' firm had decided to open a regional office near Lourdes, at Tarbes. Tarbes has an international airport. Marie pleaded with Jacques to spend at least spend one day with her in Lourdes. One day out of seven, was not much to ask.

With real misgivings, Jacques half-heartedly agreed to his wife's pleas. They boarded the plane at Orly Airport, along with two hundred pilgrims, including a number of sick and handicapped.

This is Jacques story.

"I hate crowds and hadn't been near a Church for years. Here I was catapulted into going to Lourdes for one day. My wife and I took our seats on the plane. Just in front of us I noticed a young couple with the most objectionable child I have ever seen.

The child was obviously mongol, but he was an absolute pest. The parents could hardly contain themselves at the antics of their child. The father slapped him hard, but this only seemed to increase the child's tantrums. The mother who had rather a sullen face, unkempt hair, seemed unable to cope with the child's buffoonery.

During the entire flight, the parents hardly had a moment's peace. Personally I could have quite happily strangled it. It was obvious that the parents' patience had worn down to breaking point – perhaps they thought Lourdes would provide the answer?

My one and only day in Lourdes was a tremendous penance. It was hot, the crowds enormous. I got tired standing around. I was frankly glad to return to Tarbes and set about organising the regional office. At the same time, I felt slightly deceived. At least I had gone to Lourdes, the great place of miracles, but if anything, I felt even more distanced from the church and in some respects from my wife.

At the end of the week, my wife arrived at the hotel, and we then made our way to the airport, thence to the departure lounge. It was crowded. My wife looked very happy. We boarded the plane. As I walked up the steps, I felt a certain sense of disappointment. However, at least the regional office was set up and the young manager seemed entirely competent. We took our seats and then to my horror I found we were right next to that objectionable child. His behaviour, if anything, seemed worse. Then I looked at the parents, and I couldn't believe my eyes. The mother had a serene composure about her, her eyes seemed to radiate love. She was the same person but looked entirely different. Her husband similarly seemed changed. The antics of the child somehow now seemed unimportant, because the love of the father and mother for the child completely overshadowed everything. It was strikingly obvious that something marvellous had happened internally to both parents. I looked, I stared, and then I began to cry. Just a tear at first, then a torrent. My wife held on to me; my doubts about the church, the barrier between my wife and I evaporated.

Since that air journey, I have been reconciled to the church. I attend Mass during the week, and of course I have taken over booking up our pilgrimage to Lourdes. I have found great peace and much grace. God works in strange ways."

A New Beginning

Five years ago I was living in London fifteen floors up in a tower block with my daughter, who was then four years old. I was half way through a teacher training course, and was called to the hospital to receive the results of tests taken the year before. I was greeted by a young doctor, who told me that I had Multiple Sclerosis, that there was nothing I could do about it and that I had better go home and have a good cry.

I qualified the following year and got a job teaching mentally ill adults at a workshop in central London. I found this very rewarding. When we finished for the summer break I came down to the country supposedly for a holiday with my father for a couple of weeks, and proceeded to get quite seriously ill. I was being visited by the doctor every day and it wasn't long before they brought me a wheelchair. So that was the end of London for my daughter and for me.

During the next two and a half years I received a great deal of help from the local Parish Priest, who visited me regularly during that time. He was, and still is, a tremendous support, particularly when I was fighting with my own anger and frustration at the sudden changes in my life. His care and ministry began for me the move back towards God.

At my father's suggestion I decided I would feel happier going to Lourdes rather than seeking "a cure". So we set off for Lourdes in August 1985.

I think I will leave out the details of the actual journey. Suffice it to say, for a sick pilgrim it was not easy. I began my pilgrimage wishing I had never come at all and had stayed at home. However, beneath my turbulence was a deeper knowledge that I was wanting to draw nearer to God.

The first thing that happened when we arrived was a service. The bishop gave a sermon: "We are here at Lourdes, we are here to celebrate for a week, and the most important people who are here are the sick pilgrims, not because they are ill, but because these are the people who have been chosen by God to share in part of what was Christ's suffering."

I found this message completely extraordinary. I had never heard it before, and I simply didn't understand it. We were surrounded by loving, caring people, who were doing their utmost to help us; all these people sitting around in wheelchairs and complaining! And when it finally began to penetrate, that message, I felt two things. The first was, "If it is true, then it's exciting – I have been chosen," and the second was the feeling that came later that said that I was not worthy to have been chosen. I dealt with my illness appallingly, I made other people's lives more difficult than they already were, and suddenly the task of sharing in Christ's suffering seemed too vast for me actually to have any part in at all.

Lourdes has an atmosphere which is very conducive to prayer, and I found that one of my first prayers was a deeply felt prayer asking God to remove my head! Not quite literally! But I know myself as a thinker and a worrier and I create anxieties for myself. I began doing that at Lourdes so I prayed to God to help me.

That evening we went to a candle-lit procession service, which we were leading. When the procession halted I found that I was crying. I think I must have sobbed for three possibly four hours, right through the whole service. And it wasn't until the following morning that I realised that my prayer had been answered – I can't think and cry at the same time! And also it was the answer to more. In my day to day life I had no way of expressing the grief which had been building up over the last few years. Suddenly I was expressing it and feeling better about it.

It was a strange feeling when I realised what I had been given, because I found myself praying "God, please, I have been on my own with my daughter for these last years, and I have had to organise my own life. Yes, of course I want You to be in control and I want it to be according to Your will, but please, not quite so fast, I don't think I can cope." Which, looking back on it, is a very silly prayer, but I know that's how I felt at the time – I felt quite frightened.

Then shortly afterwards I had what was for me a very unexpected experience. I realised that there was only one thing I needed to say to God, or before God, and that was "Thank you for this illness." For the first time I felt it in every bit of me. It had never occurred to me before that it was possible to thank God for something which has been both painful and extremely problematic. M.S. has not only brought me back to God, but it has brought me into contact with people who have come to help me and have given me a lot of love – longed for but not recognised in my life beforehand.

We went to a service called The International Mass. At this Mass it was arranged that all the different nationalities were mixed up together. It was taken by one of the Cardinals closest to the Pope, and there were something like 500 priests and 50 bishops.

What did I do with this very powerful service? I sat and sobbed throughout it. I was overwhelmed by a sense of my own sinfulness. Looking back I could see no point at which I hadn't been sinful. Suddenly I understood that without God there was nothing else I could be but sinful.

"O Lamb of God that takest away the sins of the World, have mercy upon me."

I sensed that I was being led. Towards what?

In preparation for the last service of this pilgrimage I went to Confession and received Absolution at the end of it, which was a marvellous feeling of suddenly being cleansed.

And then the last day and the Anointing of the Sick. I don't quite know how to describe what happened for me. The whole time I was at Lourdes I was very much as a child, and that showed itself through numerous tears and a feeling of "I don't understand anything". As a sick pilgrim I received Laying on of Hands from two priests, and then the bishop came and anointed my forehead and the palms of both my hands with oil. I found that I was filled with exaltation. I was once again crying. At each wonderful bit of the music I would burst out into tears, but tears of joy and of a real recognition.

As a child, I felt as though God had appeared to me, had looked directly at me and had said "You are loved", "You are forgiven", "You are chosen". There was nothing more to say. I felt as though a miracle had just taken place for me. I sat and cried with happiness and wonder. I have never felt so fully loved as I was at that moment.

"Love bade me welcome" praise God.

It was a shock to arrive home and find that life was exactly as I had left it. But, I had changed and I continue to be aware that I have received gifts from God, and am still receiving them. Throughout my life God is with me and has always been there when I have been most in need.

The Hospitalite

There is no English equivalent to the French word Hospitalite. The Hospitalite of Our Lady of Lourdes, is an organisation which primarily assists the sick and handicapped pilgrims. It is also responsible for the organisation of the Blessed Sacrament Procession, the Torchlight Procession, the movement of sick pilgrims to the International Masses, and unloading and loading sick pilgrims from aeroplanes and trains. It also provides men and women to work in the Baths throughout the pilgrimage year. The work is purely voluntary and unpaid. However a Brancardier or Handmaid has to undergo a period of training to enable him or her to cope with their responsibilities, and to be of service to the sick and other pilgrims.

One of the unsung miracles that occurs year in and year out is that just by chance enough men and women arrive each week at the "Hospitalite" to offer their services. If this did not happen then the whole of the Lourdes programme could come to a grinding halt. Imagine 8,000 sick pilgrims arriving each week and 40,000 ordinary pilgrims and no helpers. These Brancardier and Handmaids come from Italy, Germany, France, Spain, Portugal, Austria, the Netherlands, Belgium, England, U.S.A., South Africa, Japan – yes from all parts of the globe. Nobody knows when they are coming, but somehow they arrive at the right time in the right numbers, so that the 4-5 million pilgrims can participate in the various ceremonies.

Just one of the enjoyable parts of the day is the international lunch. 400-500 men and women from different nations sit down at trestle tables. There are two lunch sittings. The food is plain but wholesome. Generally a bishop is guest of honour, and after the main course he is invited to make an address.

On one particular day a French archbishop arrived and amid tremendous cheers (from the French) sat down at the top table. I asked why he was so popular, and I was told he was a holy Bishop, much liked in France. After the main course was finished the Archbishop rose and delivered a speech which had the French in fits of laughter. The English could not understand his jokes. After he had sat down I thought perhaps he is popular because of his gregarious bonhomie, rather than any spiritual qualities. After lunch is finished we have to take our plates into the large kitchen. I was astounded to see the archbishop elbow deep in greasy water, washing up.

I stood and watched. After a while he put on his jacket and pectoral cross, and brought all the kitchen staff together. He then said a prayer with them, blessed them and thanked them for their work and left. Perhaps the French were right about their archbishop after all!

The Children's Baths

Before passing onto the next story, I would just like to tell you about an extraordinary Italian I had the privilege to work with in the Children's Baths, perhaps the most harrowing place to assist in the whole of Lourdes.

The majority of babies and children that are brought in by their mothers are incurably ill, the only vestige of hope lies in a miraculous cure.

The mothers of these children come to Lourdes to ask God to cure their children, and it is in the Children's Baths that this request takes place in earnest. The mothers have no inhibitions; they know the reality of the situation, their plea comes from the depths of their souls. They fall on their knees, they implore Christ, through his Mother, they offer everything up, they weep tears from the heart. The sight of a mother on her knees begging God for a cure is enough to melt the hardest heart.

My Italian friend, Dondino, was a sculptor from Genoa. He stood five feet two inches tall, black hair, and thirty years old a father of two. There was nothing exceptional about him, that is until he started to sing. As the mother and child entered Dondino began to hum, then when the mother started to pray for the child, Dondino began to sing, he always sang the "Ave Maria". Amidst the cries for help from the mother, usually joined by the noisier crying of the baby, the beautiful prayer began to overshadow the particular human suffering. Gradually a calmness descended upon the mother. It was as if in some unfathomable way in a moment in eternity, her prayer had been answered. Every mother that left the Baths left in a spirit of tranquillity.

"Que soy era Immaculada Councepciou"
"I am the Immaculate Conception"

The Grotto of Massabielle

The Blessed Sacrament Procession

The Holy Father John Paul II
praying at the Grotto

The blessing of the sick pilgrims

The torchlight procession

The international Mass, in the underground Basilica
dedicated to St Pius X

A view of the Rosary Basilica, the Crypt, the Upper Basilica

The Fountains. "Go and drink from the spring and wash yourself there."

"Go and tell the priest to build a chapel here."

Bernadette Soubirous
(1861)

Bernadette incorrupt

Coincidences

You can remember quite vividly when someone important to you forgets your birthday. The pain and sadness of being forgotten is heightened in direct proportion to the relationship you have with that person. Imagine the anguish felt by a child whose mother has forgotten his or her birthday.

It is inconceivable that a sick pilgrim could be forgotten in Lourdes? But that is what appeared to happen to Casey Phillips.

This is his story.

I suffered a stroke fifteen years ago at the age of 22. I was suddenly paralysed down one side of my body. I speak with great difficulty. At a stroke my entire life changed – I used to play on the left wing for our league football teams. I was the assistant manager in my uncle's butcher's shop, and I had decided to ask Julia if she would marry me. The stroke ruined my life. All my hopes and expectations for the future vanished in one black moment. To begin with everyone was very sorry and helpful, but after a while my friends' visits became more and more infrequent. Julie was kind and attentive, but soon found another boy friend. I felt that I had become a liability to those around me, and I became a bitter man. Every day I asked the question "why did this happen to me – why me?" I used to shake my fist at God, and I blamed God for my illness. When you become morose and bitter your popularity soon dwindles. The only people who spoke to me were the care assistants and nurses in the home, my only friend the Matron was leaving for Australia. At the age of 38 I felt a forgotten, unwanted man, useless to society and a burden on the state. Then I was invited to go on a pilgrimage to Lourdes.

This pilgrimage to Lourdes was a godsend. It brought some relief to my humdrum existence in the Nursing Home in Lancashire. New faces, a different language, people to talk to, wine and of course sunshine. As you can have gathered I was not religious.

On the third day of the pilgrimage, we were taken to the International Mass in the Underground Basilica. The place was packed, and it soon became stuffy. I am able to propel myself for a very short distance, with my good right hand. I saw a large space close to one of the pillars. I moved out of the packed wheel chair line and positioned myself by the pillar. By the end of the Mass I had become hot, and thirsty, and my body was aching from sitting in the chair for over two hours.

There were seven thousand sick in stretchers, and wheelchairs waiting patiently to be moved. The sacristan had begun switching off the lights. I had been in the very last row of wheelchairs. Eventually everyone disappeared. I waited, surely someone would come for me. I moved away from the pillar. I waited. It began to dawn on me that I really had been forgotten – I had been left behind. My emotions began to overwhelm me, I realised that even here in Lourdes, this holy place, the place of Mary, the town of miracles, the city of grace, here above all places I was forgotten. I buried my hands in my face. Then something quite remarkable happened. It was not dramatic or miraculous, but extraordinary.

I heard footsteps, I looked up, and in the gloom I saw two people approaching, one of whom was a nurse. The man came up to me, he could see my distressed condition. He put his arm around me and said "I have come back for you, I'm sorry I'm late. My name is Casey". He showed me his name printed on a card which was pinned to his jacket. I of course couldn't speak, because I was upset, but I pointed to my hospital label. My name also was printed "Casey" Phillips. What an extraordinary coincidence of the 50,000 or so people in Lourdes, a brancardier with the same name as mine came back for me. The nurse began to make me more comfortable. She was about my age with dark hair and eyes. She soon found out about my illness. She asked me where I lived, and I told her. "Casey," she said, "before coming to Lourdes I was appointed to be the Matron of a hospital near your Nursing Home". I was dumbfounded. These coincidences were too much to hear, I couldn't believe it, first the coincidence of the names, and now the coincidence of the nurse who would be near the Nursing Home. All these thoughts were chasing through my head as we went back to the hospital. That afternoon Casey and Aileen were back to see me and took me to one of the cafes in the town. They both became my great friends in Lourdes. On the last day I asked Aileen to take me to the Grotto – I looked up at the statue of Mary and said "So you hadn't forgotten me after all." I swear that the statue seemed to smile down at me.

I now feel wanted, my life has changed. Perhaps the most remarkable thing of all is that my best friend hangs on a cross. He and I have a lot in common, and now I don't blame him any more for my illness. I have found a new life and oddly enough it is based on love – the love of God, and my fellowmen. Aileen looks after me and Casey visits me from time to time. I often think of that remarkable set of coincidences and how they changed my life. Outwardly everything is still the same, but if you could see inside me you would not recognise me. Bitterness has been transformed into love.

Arrested in Lourdes

One of our priests, a monsignor, decided that he would like to hear confessions. So on this particular warm August day he presented himself at the "Chapel de Reconciliation", and was duly installed in one of the confessionals. In this Chapel there are about 35 confessionals. Above each confessional is a notice stating the language the confession will be heard in. The main languages being French, Italian, Spanish, Portuguese, German, Dutch and English. Other languages are also catered for including Eastern European languages.

Our Monsignor heard some forty confessions, and then there was a lull in the proceedings. Although he could hear noises outside, people genuflecting and whispering, he did not know that all the English pilgrims had departed. It grew warm in the confessional and the Monsignor closed his eyes and went to sleep.

When he awoke the place was in complete darkness. Immediately he stood up and turned the handle of the door and it broke in his hand. He was locked in. Our Monsignor, a resourceful cleric, decided to exit the confessional through the roof. He pushed upwards and the roof came off. He removed his stole, his jacket and Roman collar and with consummate skill climbed out of the confessional, and lowered himself to the ground. Having accomplished this remarkable climbing feat, he found his way to the main door and started banging on it. Just outside the Chapel, there is often a Gendarme on duty. The Gendarme heard this banging. Eventually a sacristan arrived with the key and they found a middle aged gentleman clad in trousers and white shirt claiming to be a Monsignor. The Gendarme decided it would be best if all the explanations took place at the police station. The Monsignor said to me later – "I go to Lourdes on pilgrimage and get arrested after hearing confessions. I wonder what the tabloid press would have made of it?"

The Polish Question

My husband died suddenly five years ago, from a colossal heart attack. Prior to his death, we had planned to visit Lourdes. It took me over two years to get over this tragic loss, but time is a good healer. I have two chil-dren. My married daughter aged 28 has one child. Her husband has left her, and I have not spoken to her for two years. Her carelessness caused the death of my grandson, who was the image of my husband. She had failed to put the car seat belt around him, when collect-ing him from school. He went straight through the windscreen. She lives in a council flat in Bourne-mouth. My son, a city analyst, is doing very well on the Stock Exchange. He lives with a very pretty girl in St John's Wood.

I had become self indulgent (well why not). I love being pampered again. Krabuc used to pamper me, he left me a rich woman. I revelled in the luxury of being free to do precisely what pleased me. I could afford the best of everything. My yearly calendar was divided between cruises, staying with friends in Cali-fornia, the Chelsea flat and my seaside home. At Christmas I received a letter from my daughter, as soon as I recognised the writing on the envelope, I tore it up and told my maid to burn it.

My year was precisely organised, except for one week in July. It was then I decided to visit Lourdes in memory of my husband. The Travel Agent booked me into the best hotel. What I could not know was that my arrival in Lourdes coincided with the first

Polish pilgrimage to Lourdes since the Second World War. That pilgrimage was to upset my whole life. This is how events unfolded.

The communist authorities had finally relented and allowed a group of Catholics to come by train. The train journey through Poland had taken four days, this was due to the deliberate delaying tactics the communists employed. There were 100 pilgrims composed of 2 priests, 4 doctors, 11 nurses, 10 'helpers', and 73 sick pilgrims, of which one was a stretcher case.

There was great jubilation as the train pulled into Lourdes. However the authorities were appalled that there were so few 'able' Polish pilgrims to cope with so many sick! The doctors later explained, "we were only allowed to bring one hundred, so we decided to bring as many sick as possible"

A serious problem soon manifested itself. The Polish pilgrims could not speak any French or English, communication was extremely difficult. It was heightened by the overwhelming concern of the doctors to have the sick Poles transported to one of the Lourdes' hospitals. With gesticulations accompanied with much arm waving, the pilgrimage made its way out of the station.

Whilst this drama was developing, I was sitting in the lounge of the hotel, sipping a glass of white wine. A priest came striding into the lounge. He stopped, looked around, then said "May I have your attention. A Polish pilgrimage has arrived in Lourdes, we are seeking an interpreter. Does anyone here speak Polish?" I said nothing, but saw that a number of people were looking at me. Then someone whispered to the priest and pointed at me. The priest came over. "I understand you are Polish." "Yes Father, but please

– I don't want to get involved. Please try and find someone else." The priest sat down beside me. "All we want you to do is to interpret for us. We need to explain to the doctors, the various medical facilities that are available. They need a programme in Polish, giving times of the various services, processions, where the priests can celebrate mass. Perhaps just an hour of your time each day, whilst you are in Lourdes?" I stood up "Father, I am here on a private visit in memory of my husband – I cannot help you." The priest stared at me, my black silk suit, my pearl necklace. The large diamond on my right hand, seemed to speak volumes. "You are right", he said, "The Poles would be better off without someone like you." I was speechless – no-one had ever spoken to me like that, especially a priest. He strode out of the hotel. I was furious, I decided to follow, I would give him a piece of my mind. The priest had long strides. I couldn't catch him, and I certainly wasn't going to run. He turned into the St Frai hospital. I kept him in sight. He went up a flight of stairs and turned right. I followed and suddenly found myself in the middle of a ward, people lying all over the place, the smell was frightful.

"The children's ward is on the next floor". The man pointed upwards. Then the doctor replied in Polish "I don't understand you". I turned to the doctor. "The children's ward is on the first floor". He threw his arms around me. "Our interpreter – thank God you have arrived." What could I do, I was trapped. The doctor took my arm and smiled, "Please come with me". I spent the rest of the evening until midnight with the pilgrimage, and was back at the hospital at 7 am the following morning. The black silk suit had been replaced by trousers and a tee-shirt. I began to meet the sick pilgrims. One of the nurses asked me where my home town was in Poland, and I told her I had been born just outside of Gdansk at Zappot. My father had worked in the shipyard. The nurse said "We have a boy from Gdansk, he is nearly nine, but he has a kidney disease. Would you like to meet him?" Krasnik was small for his age, under-weight, with large blue eyes. He had a sad face. The nurse said "Krasnik is an orphan".

After two days with the Poles, spending 8-10 hours a day with them, I began to go to their services. I had attended Mass about once a month, and hadn't been to confession for three years. Krasnik seemed to have at-tached himself to me, he could walk short distances, but was generally pushed around in a wheel chair. On the fourth day we were to have a concelebrated Mass with a Dutch pilgrimage at the Grotto. That morning, there was a shortage of wheel chairs. At last everyone was accommodated, except for young Krasnik. One of the doctor's said "I will go back for him", I said "No you won't, I will." I left the Grotto, running some of the way back to the hospital, pushing an empty wheel chair. Krasnik was waiting, a great smile spread over his face, when he saw me approach.

We went down through the Domaine to the Grotto, where Mass had started. There was a great sense of peace, of joy, of tranquillity. I looked at the niche where the statue of Mary rested. The priest had started to preach in Polish. "She is the Mother of the Church, the Mother of Poland, and our heavenly Mother." Krasnik was looking at the statue, then he looked at me, there were tears in his eyes. It was at this moment something happened, as if my eyes were opened for the first time in my life, I felt entirely different, but then I seemed to be looking at myself, my conceit, my egotism, my vanity, my worldliness. I had become totally self centred. I had abandoned my only daughter, and had virtually given up my faith. I began to weep, and then I asked the Mother of God to help me. I don't know how or what prompted me, but I took Krasnik in my arms and said to him "Can I be your mother?" He buried his head on my shoulders.

After the Mass I took Krasnik back to the hospital, his hand in mine. It would have taken the strength of Hercules to separate us. I told the doctors and the priest what I had said to Krasnik. They were smiling hugely as if they were sharing a secret. "He needs a liver transplant, his treatment is very costly. We need permission for you to take him to England – the Polish authorities may prove difficult. There are many very serious problems to overcome." If there is one thing I have learnt, that is, problems have a habit of disappearing in the face of 'money'. That was a commodity in abundance.

As soon as I got back to the hotel, I telephoned my son and told him what had happened, and asked him for my daughter's telephone number. He told me that Janice was not on the phone, so I sent a telegram. It read "Please forgive me, your real mother returns to England from Lourdes. Try and meet me at the airport. I was blind, now I can see. Your mother loves you and needs you both."

As we were leaving to go to the airport, the doctors, nurses and priests of the pilgrimage came to say goodbye to Krasnik and to me. The priest said "One of our novenas before coming out to Lourdes was for Krasnik, that Our Lady would help him. Well she hasn't done badly. He has a new mother, a Polish mother at that, and he is going to receive expert medical attention, and he is going to be loved."

My whole life changed since that visit to Lourdes. My daughter was reconciled to her husband and lives near me; my son has married and has two children. All the grandchildren are young men and women now. And Krasnik was ordained to the priesthood on my 65th birthday.

Casimir's Cure

The first symptoms of our son's illness appeared in October-December 1964, mainly as general tiredness and headaches. These increased gradually and early in 1965 were accompanied by sleepiness and vomiting.

On the 1st April our son was admitted to Bromley Hospital for examination and later transferred to Brooks Regional Hospital and Guy Maudsley Neurosurgical Unit, where the illness was diagnosed as Glioma and Astrocytoma in the neck region – apparently incurable diseases.

At the beginning of May a double vision appeared. On 4th May a biopsy and some emptying of cysts was carried out. The biopsy confirmed the diagnosis and also considerable extent of the tumour – some 11 cm long located between the nervous cords, therefore completely inaccessible and impossible to treat by surgical methods.

Kazimierz (Casimir, my son's name) had slightly improved after the emptying of the cysts as was expected. He was then transferred to Guy's hospital for a course (30 sessions) of hard X-ray irradiations. During this treatment his condition started to deteriorate again and at the end of June he had marked difficulty in exercising muscular control, double vision, speech difficulties, some nausea and change of taste – most fruits appeared salty to him.

After the irradiation he was transferred to Brooks Hospital and then quite unexpectedly discharged on the Feast of Our Lady of Carmel, 16th July.

From subsequent enquiries it appeared that the irradiation was ineffective. This was confirmed by his continuous worsening, difficulty in swallowing, frequent violent vertigo, even when lying in bed, acute double vision. During a check-up in Guy's Hospital (6th August 1965) the advance of the tumour was confirmed; it was extending now to the cerebellum. During this visit the examining doctor filled in the Sick Pilgrim's form for Lourdes; this form should still be with the Catholic Association.

In the course of the next few days his condition deteriorated so rapidly that one of our main thoughts was "How is he going to survive until September" (the time of our pilgrimage to Lourdes 3rd-11th September 1965)?

Our Lady gave us her reply.

On the 10th August a fairly high fever appeared (103.5) and Kazimierz was unable to swallow even liquid medicines. His breathing was difficult and painful and the pulse irregular.

Our doctor – very alarmed – insisted on hospitalisation, as the state was clearly critical. The boy was instantly admitted to Bromley Hospital and treated for bronco-pneumonia, which had developed as a secondary consequence of the tumour.

On the day of his admission I wrote a letter to Bishop W. Rubin, who baptized our son in 1947 and is now a bishop – delegate to all Poles abroad and a Secretary of the Synod of Bishops in Rome. Bishop Rubin was leading the Polish National Pilgrimage to Lourdes (13th-17th August) and I asked him to intercede with Our Lady for Kazimierz.

Between 10th and 14th the boy's condition remained fairly static or slightly improved: the fever subsided and he could swallow small quantities of liquids. On 14th (Saturday) however an irregularity of the pulse had increased, a doctor visited several times during the night; we ourselves half expected to be called to our son during the night also. In Lourdes (we learnt later) Bishop Rubin and another priest said Masses with the Polish pilgrims for Kazimierz's intentions and we kept a complete fast all day on the Vigil of the Assumption of Our Lady and to commemorate the anniversary of the death of Fr Maximilian Kolbe, a martyr in Auschwitz for another prisoner. Fr Kolbe had the greatest devotion to the Immaculate Conception and made enormous efforts to spread love of her in Poland and Japan.

On Sunday, 15th August, when my wife went to visit our son – he was sitting up in his bed and eating his lunch with the greatest appetite. Virtually all major symptoms had disappeared, he was bright and joyful – we couldn't believe our eyes.

His condition was such that he was discharged from the hospital on 19th – exactly nine days after his admission and at the end of a novena which we started to Fr Kolbe on the day of his departure.

When we started on our way to Lourdes he was not yet completely well. The journey was quite tiring and on the first day he was on a stretcher. On the next day a wheelchair was enough and on the third day he walked unaided to the Grotto and back. He was walking all day on Our Lady's birthday – her gift to us. He is well ever since, sitting for his "A" levels this June (Maths, French, History), playing with his peers and leading a completely normal life. As you know, in 1966, in Lourdes, he was a brancardier and we hope it will be the same this year.

I Met a Miracle

Fr Patrick O'Connor

On Friday morning, 10th September 1937, I came face to face with a miracle. The meeting place was a bustling railway station in France. There was no mistaking the miracle, as with the weight and strength of sixteen stone of burly humanity it helped me to fight my way on to a crowded train.

The name of the miracle was John Traynor. I first beheld him as I came along the platform with my suitcase and saw him waiting to board the coach in which I hoped to ride. A powerfully built man, about five feet ten in height, with a strong, wholesome, ruddy face, dressed in a rather rumpled grey suit, carrying his travelling bag, he stood out from the surrounding crowd. Two of his little boys were with him, and eight or ten Irish and English pilgrims on their way home from Lourdes.

Now John Traynor was a miracle because, by all the laws of nature, he should not have been standing there, hefty and healthy. He should have been, if alive at all, paralysed, epileptic, a mass of sores, shrunken, with a shrivelled, useless right arm and a gaping hole in his skull. That is what he had been. That is the way medical skill had had to leave him, after making its best efforts. That is the way medical science had certified that he must remain. Only a miracle could cure him... A miracle did.

I rode with him for about ten hours in the train that day, and when I said good-bye to him in Paris that evening, it was with the certainty that I could never forget him. He was a delightful character, this big Liverpool Irishman, with his manly faith and piety, lacking all trace of exaggeration in one direction or the other; unaffected and unassuming, yet obviously a fearless militant Catholic; with only a primary education but with a clear mind enriched by the faith and preserved by a great honesty of life. Not for his personality, however, am I bound to remember him but for his story, which he told me on our long journey that day. He told it simply, soberly, exactly, a narrative that it was a grace to hear and is a duty to recall.

Verified

Afterwards I wrote it down and sent my version back to him for checking. Painstakingly, with the aid of Mr John Murray, the old schoolmaster who had taught him as a boy in St Patrick's School, he went over the manuscript, correcting, filling in gaps, adding details. I had the files of the Liverpool newspapers searched to find the corroborative evidence of their reports. I obtained copies of newspaper photographs taken at the time of the miracle. I read the official report signed by six doctors, four English, one French and one Belgian, and issued by the Medical Bureau in Lourdes when more than three years elapsed to allow for careful examination of all the evidence and to establish the permanence of the cure.

And now, here is the story of John Traynor.

John Traynor was born and reared in Liverpool. His Irish mother died when he was still quite young, but her faith, her devotion to Mass and Holy Communion and her trust in the Blessed Mother stayed with him as a memory and a fruitful example. "She was a daily communicant when few people were," he told me.

In the First World War

The First World War broke out in 1914, and Jack Traynor was mobilized with the Royal Naval Reserve, to which he belonged. He was in the naval brigade that took part in the unsuccessful Antwerp expedition of October 1914, and was in the last battalion to retreat. He was carrying one of his officers to safety, when he was hit on the head by shrapnel. He did not regain consciousness until five weeks later, when he woke up after an operation in a marine hospital in England. He recovered rapidly and went back into service. In 1915, lent to the 1st Dublin Fusiliers, as physical instructor, he was a member of the expeditionary force sent to Egypt and the Dardanelles.

On 25th April 1915, he took part in the landing from the steamship River Clyde at Gallipoli. He was in charge of the first boat to leave the ship and was one of the few to reach the shore that day. From their positions in the steep banks above the beach the Turks raked the Clyde and the boats with deadly gun-fire. The casualties were so heavy that the operation was suspended until nightfall. Meanwhile all the officers in the landing parties had been killed, and Traynor found himself in charge of about 100 men, who took cover in a shallow trench. A Catholic chaplain, Fr Finn, was killed in the second boat, from which he fell. Traynor dragged him from under the barbed wire and later he and his comrades buried him on shore.

After dusk more officers men landed, and the small force began to fight its way, with severe losses, up to the sand hills. For days the bitter fighting continued. Traynor took part, without injury, until 8th May when he was hit by machine-gun fire during a bayonet charge.

He seems to have been literally sprayed with bullets. He was wounded in the head and chest, while a bullet tore through the inner side of his upper right arm and lodged under the collarbone.

Medical corps men brought him back, dazed and suffering, to the beach, and he was shipped to the base hospital at Alexandria, Egypt. Now began his long years as an invalid and as the patient of unsuccessful operations. A well – known English surgeon, Sir Frederick Treves, operated on him in Alexandria, in an attempt to sew together the severed nerves in the upper arm, which the bullet wound had left paralysed and useless. The attempt failed, and so did another, made by another surgeon, on the hospital ship that brought Traynor from Alexandria to England. In September 1915, in the Haslar naval hospital, England, a third operation was performed with the same object – and the same result.

While on the hospital ship Traynor suffered his first epileptic attack. These attacks became frequent.

Incurable

The surgeon-general of the navy now advised amputation of the paralysed arm, as there seemed to be no hope of ever joining the torn and shrunken nerves. Traynor would not consent. In November 1916, another doctor tried to suture the nerves, bringing the number of unsuccessful operations up to four. By this time Traynor had been discharged from the service, first on 80 per cent pension, then on 100 per cent as being permanently and completely disabled. He had to spend months in various hospitals as an epileptic patient. In April 1920, a doctor realised that the epilepsy was probably the result of the head wounds, and operated on the skull. Whether bits of shrapnel were found and removed is not known, but we do know that the operation left Traynor with an open hole about an inch wide in his skull. Through this opening the pulsations of the brain could be observed. A silver plate was inserted to shield the brain. The epileptic condition was no better after the operation. The fits were as frequent as three a day. Both legs were partly paralysed, and nearly every organ in Traynor's body was impaired.

An ambulance brought him back to Liverpool, where he lived with his wife and children in a house in Grafton Street. "We were very poor," he told me. The Ministry of Pensions supplied him with a wheelchair; in this he would sit for hours outside the house. He had to be lifted from his bed into the chair and back again.

The year 1923 – the eighth after he became a casualty in Gallipoli – found him leading this helpless existence. I have counted the names of ten doctors through whose hands he had passed up to then. The result of all their efforts and examinations was to prove that he was completely and incurably incapacitated. Unable to stand or walk, subject to frequent epileptic fits, with three open wounds, one of them in his head, without the power of feeling or movement in his torn and shrivelled right arm, he was indeed a human wreck. Somebody arranged to have him admitted to the Mossley Hill Hospital for Incurables on 24th July 1923. But by that date Jack Traynor was to be in Lourdes.

What follows is his own narrative, as I wrote it down and as he checked it.

John Traynor's Narrative

I had always had a great devotion to our Blessed Lady, having acquired it from my mother especially. I felt now that if Our Lady's shrine at Lourdes was in England, I would go there often. But it seemed to be a faraway place that I could never reach.

In the month of July 1923, I was at home, helpless as usual, when a neighbour woman came into the house and spoke of an announcement that had been made in our parish. A Liverpool diocesan pilgrimage was being organised for Lourdes. It would cost thirteen pounds to go. A down payment of one pound would engage a place.

My wife was out in the yard and I called her in. I found afterwards that she had already heard about the pilgrimage, but had decided not to tell me, fearing that I'd want to go. I told her to go upstairs and get a certain box in which we kept a gold sovereign, which my brother had given me and which we were treasuring for some special emergency. She asked me what I wanted to do with it now. I said that I wanted to give it to Mrs Cunningham, a neighbour, as a first payment on a ticket to Lourdes. My wife was very disturbed, but finally did as I told her, and the neighbour went off to make the booking for me.

A few days later, one of the priests in charge of the pilgrimage came to see me. He was upset at the thought of my going and wanted me to cancel my booking.

"You cannot make the trip," he said. "You will die on the way and bring trouble and grief to everybody."

My answer was that I had made my first payment, I had booked my place and I was going to Lourdes!

After much talking, he said finally: "Well, you won't be allowed to travel unless the doctor gives his approval. If you get a medical certificate, we'll take you." Clearly he seemed to think that it was impossible.

I thought that my doctor would approve of the trip, but he refused. We called in several doctors and every one of them said that it would be suicide. Later, when the Ministry of Pensions learned that I had gone to Lourdes, they protested very strongly.

The priest came again to visit me and flung himself across my bed, begging me to give up the idea. I would not – and finally succeeded in going without any medical certificate. To raise the twelve pounds, the balance due on my ticket, we sold some of our belongings and my wife pawned even her few bits of jewellery.

By this time it had got around Liverpool that this crippled and paralysed ex-serviceman wanted to go to Lourdes, and the papers began to write about it. I was the centre of more attention than I liked. Everybody, with the exception of my wife and one or two relatives, told me I was crazy.

Departure for Lourdes

The day for leaving Liverpool came. The pilgrims were to travel on two trains. It was a terrible task to prepare me. I hardly realised what the journey was, and I had nothing I could take with me, except the few shillings left over after we had paid for the ticket. My wife lifted me out of bed, and my brother Francis got me into my invalid chair. There I remained, while the others attended the 4 am Mass at St Malachy's. Then, rushed and excited and hoping to avoid public notice, they raced me down through all the back streets of Liverpool to get me to the station.

At the station, there was a large crowd of pilgrims and their friends. Already my case was well known through the newspapers, and people began to fuss around us, making it still more difficult for me to get to the platform. I did reach it – just too late! The first train was about to leave. The priest-director came up to me in great agitation and said: "Traynor, you're too late! We can't get you on the train now. In Heaven's name, take this as a sign that you are not to come. You will only die on the journey."

I said: "Father, I have paid for my ticket to Lourdes and I'm going to Lourdes."

He said: "You'll die on the way."

I said: "Then I'll die in a good cause."

There was another train, and I said that they could put me in the coal tender or anywhere they liked, as long as they put me on the train. By being obstinate about it, I won my point, was placed on the second train amid scenes of excitement and confusion, and began my journey to Lourdes.

In 1923 arrangements for taking care of the sick on the English pilgrimages to Lourdes were not by any means as good as they were later on. The experience was very trying.

I remember practically nothing of the journey, except seeing a number of sick people on stretchers beside me on platforms and docks, some of them bleeding, all of them suffering. I believe that I was very sick on the way. Three times they tried to take me off the train in France to bring me to a hospital, as I seemed to be dying. Each time there was no hospital where they stopped, and the only thing to do was to go on again, with me still on board.

At Lourdes

We reached Lourdes on 22nd July and I was transferred with the rest of the sick to the Asile Hospital in the domain of the Grotto. I was in a terrible condition, as my wounds and sores had not been freshly bandaged since I left Liverpool.

Meanwhile a Protestant girl from Liverpool had come to the Continent on a holiday tour. She got tired of all the usual show places and happened to come to Lourdes. She was a trained nurse and, seeing all the sick, she offered her services to help in the Asile. Her parents in England, upset at her decision to stay as a volunteer worker in Lourdes, sent out her sister to keep her company. These two girls went down to see the Liverpool pilgrims. They remembered having seen me sitting in my wheelchair outside my house at home and they volunteered to take care of me. I gladly accepted their kind offer, and they washed and dressed my sores and looked after me during my stay in Lourdes.

Ours was a large pilgrimage, comprising about 1,200 people in all, including many priests, headed by the late Archbishop Keating of Liverpool. We spent six days in Lourdes. During that time I was desperately ill. I had several haemorrhages as well as epileptic fits. In fact, one woman took it upon herself to write to my wife, saying that there was no hope for me and that I'd be buried in Lourdes.

In spite of my condition, however, I succeeded in being bathed nine times in the water from the Grotto spring and I was taken to the different devotions in which the sick could join. On the morning of the second day I had a bad epileptic fit as I was being wheeled to the baths. Blood flowed from my mouth and the doctors were very much alarmed. As I came to, I could hear them saying: "Better take him back to the Asile at once."

I protested, saying: "No, you won't. I've come to be bathed and I'm not going back."

"You'll die in the bath," they told me.

"Very well," I said. "If I do, I'll die in a good place."

I put the brake on the wheelchair by holding the wheel with my good hand, the left one, and the brancardiers (volunteer stretcher-bearers) had to give in. They took me into the bath and bathed me in the usual way. I never had an epileptic fit after that.

Medical Examination

On 24th July Drs Azurdia, Finn and Marley, who had come with the pilgrimage, examined Traynor at Lourdes. Their signed statement is on record. It testifies that they found him to be suffering from:

1. Epilepsy ("We ourselves saw several attacks during his journey to Lourdes");
2. Paralysis of the radial, median and ulnar nerves of the right arm;

3. Atrophy of the shoulder and pectoral muscles;
4. A trephine opening in the right parietal region of the skull; in this opening, about 2.5 cm., there is a metal plate for protection;
5. Absence of voluntary movement in the legs and loss of feeling;
6. Lack of bodily control.

We were to leave on the morning of 27th July. The afternoon of 25th July came and I seemed to be as bad as ever. Already preparations were being made for the return journey. A young Frenchman, Felix Douly, who used to come to the Asile selling rosaries and medals, came into our ward, and the last few shillings I had I spent on little religious souvenirs for my wife and children. Then it was time to get ready for the baths.

Miracle

I was wheeled down to wait my turn. There were many to be bathed and we all wanted to be finished before the afternoon procession of the Blessed Sacrament, which began at four o'clock. My turn came, and when I was in the bath, my paralysed legs became violently agitated. The brancardiers became alarmed once more, thinking that I was in another fit. I struggled to get on my feet, feeling that I could easily do so, and wondered why everybody seemed to be against me. When I was taken out of the bath, I cried from sheer weakness and exhaustion.

The brancardiers threw my clothes on hurriedly, put me back on the stretcher and rushed me down to the square in front of the Rosary Church to await the procession. Practically all the other sick were already lined up. I was the third last on the outside, to the right as you face the church.

The procession came winding its way back, as usual, to the church, and at the end walked the Archbishop of Rheims, carrying the Blessed Sacrament. He blessed the two ahead of me, came to me, made the sign of the cross with the monstrance and moved on to the next. He had just passed by when I realised that a great change had taken place in me. My right arm, which had been dead since 1915, was violently agitated. I burst its bandages and blessed myself – for the first time in years.

I had no sudden pain that I can recall and certainly had no vision. I simply realised that something momentous had happened.

I attempted to rise from my stretcher, but the brancardiers were watching me. I suppose I had a bad name for my obstinacy. They held me down and a doctor or a nurse gave me a hypo. Apparently they thought that I was hysterical and about to create a scene. Immediately after the final Benediction they rushed me back to the Asile. I told them that I could walk, and proved it by taking seven steps. I was very tired and in pain. they put me back in bed and gave me another hypo after a while.

(Drs Azurdia, Finn and Marley certify that they examined Traynor on his return to the Asile after the procession of the Blessed Sacrament. apparently this was to see if he could really walk, as he claimed. "We find that he has recovered the voluntary use of his legs; the reflexes exist. There is intense venous congestion of both feet, which are very painful. The patient can walk with difficulty.")

They had me in a small ward on the ground floor.

As I was such a troublesome case, they stationed brancardiers in relays to watch me and keep me from doing anything foolish. Late that night they placed a brancardier on guard outside the door of the ward. There were two other sick men in the room, including one who was blind.

The effect of the hypos began to wear off during the night, but I had no full realisation that I was cured. I was awake for most of the night. No lights were on.

Miracle made manifest

The chimes in the basilica above the Rosary Basilica rang the hours and half-hours as usual through the night, playing the air of the Lourdes Ave Maria.

Early in the morning I heard them ringing, and it seemed to me that I fell asleep at the beginning of the Ave. It could have been a matter of only a few seconds, but at the last stroke I opened my eyes and jumped out of bed. First, I knelt on the floor to finish the rosary I had been saying, then I dashed for the door, pushed aside the two brancardiers and ran out into the passage and the open air. Previously I had been watching the brancardiers and planning to evade them. I may say here that I had not walked since 1915 and my weight was down to eight stone.

Dr Marley was outside the door. When he saw the man over whom he had been watching during the pilgrimage, and whose death he had expected, push two brancardiers aside and run out of the ward, he fell back in amazement. Out in the open now, I ran towards the Grotto, which is about two or three hundred yards from the Asile. This stretch of ground was gravelled then, not paved, and I was barefoot. I ran the whole way to the Grotto without getting the least mark or cut on my bare feet. The brancardiers were running after me but they could not catch up with me. When they reached the Grotto, there I was on my knees, still in my night clothes, praying to Our Lady and thanking her. All I knew as that I should thank her and the Grotto was the place to do it. The brancardiers stood back, afraid to touch me.

The news was beginning to spread, even though it was still early in the morning. After I had prayed for about twenty minutes, I got up surprised and not pleased to find a crowd of people gathered around, watching me. They drew aside to let me pass, as I walked back towards the Asile. At the far end of Rosary Square stands the statue of Our Lady crowned. My mother had always taught me that when you ask a favour from Our Lady or wish to show her some special veneration you should make a sacrifice. I had no money to offer, as I had spent my last few shillings on rosaries and medals for my wife and children, but kneeling there before the Blessed Mother, I made the only sacrifice I could think of. I resolved to give up cigarettes. All this time, while knowing that I had received a great favour from Our Lady, I had no clear recollection of all the illness that had gone before.

By now the hotels of Lourdes were emptying themselves, and a crowd of excited people had gathered in front of the Asile. I could not understand what they were doing there, as I went in to dress. I put my clothes on, in a hurry, but kept away from the bed, for fear those doctors and brancardiers would tackle me again and treat me as a sick man once more.

I went to the washroom to wash and shave. Other men were there before me. I bade them all good morning, but none of them answered me – they just looked at me in a scared way. I wondered why.

It was still pretty early in the morning when a priest, Fr Gray, who knew nothing about my cure, entered the ward where I was asked if anybody could serve Mass. I answered that I would be glad to, and went off and served his Mass in the chapel of the Asile. It did not seem strange to me then that I could do this, after being unable to stand or walk for eight years.

I went in to breakfast in the dining-room of the Asile. The other men drew back, as if they were afraid of me. I could not grasp the situation nor could I understand why people were staring at me so hard. After breakfast, when I tried to walk out from the Asile, I found a large crowd outside. They made a rush for me, and I had to retreat, going into the little enclosure, feeling rather upset.

A Mr Cunningham came out to talk to me. I could see that he found it hard to control his excitement.

He said: "Good morning, Jack. Are you feeling all right?"

"Yes, Mr Cunningham," I answered "quite all right. Are you feeling all right?" Then I asked: "What are all those people doing outside?"

"They're there, Jack, because they're glad to see you."

"Well, it's very nice of them and I'm glad to see them, but I wish they'd leave me alone."

He told me that one of the priests on the pilgrimage – the one who had opposed my coming – was anxious to speak to me. He was in his hotel in the town, and the problem was how to get to him through the crowd. Finally somebody got an open, horse-drawn carriage into the enclosure in front of the Asile. Mr Cunningham and I sat in the carriage, and the old French driver started off. But the horse had taken only a few paces when the crowd surged up against the carriage in such a way that the drive was afraid to go any further. We had to get out and go back to the Asile.

Finally, after appeals to the crowd, I got through in another carriage, which brought me up to the hotel where I found the priest. He too, asked me if I was all right. I was quite surprised by the question. I told him that I felt quite well thanks, and that I hoped he did, too. He broke down and began to cry.

That day was a nightmare of excitement and crowds. I was the centre of attraction for all the people in Lourdes, it seemed to me.

We left on the nine o'clock train next morning, 27th July. I found that a first-class compartment had been set aside for me. I protested against taking it but I had to give in.

(Early in the morning of 27th July the three doctors examined Traynor before the pilgrimage left Lourdes. Their statement says that:

1. He can walk perfectly;
2. He has recovered the use and function of his right arm;
3. He has recovered sensation in his legs;
4. The opening in his skull has diminished considerably;

There have been no more epileptic crises.

When Traynor took off the last of his bandages on returning from the Grotto on the morning of 26th July, he found every one of his sores healed.)

The train went up through France, and I was still

in a sort of daze. At one of the stops, the door of my compartment opened, and to my amazement I saw the red skull-cap of Archbishop Keating. He came up into the compartment and I knelt to get his blessing. He raised me up, saying: "John, I think I should be getting your blessing." I could not understand why he said that. Then he led me over, and we both sat down on the bed. Looking at me, he said:

"John, do you realise how ill you have been and that you have been miraculously cured by the Blessed Virgin?"

Then everything came back to me, the memory of my years of illness and the sufferings of the journey to Lourdes and how ill I had been in Lourdes itself. I began to cry, and the Archbishop began to cry, and we both sat there, crying like two children. After a little talk with him, I felt composed. Now I realised fully what had happened.

Arriving Home

Meanwhile the news of the miracle had been telegraphed to the Liverpool papers, but my wife had not heard of it. Somebody on the train – Fr Quinlan or Fr McKinley – said to me that I should send her a wire. I did not care to make a fuss in a telegram, so I just sent her this message: "Am better – Jack."

One of the priests in our parish, Fr Dawber, got the news from the papers and rushed down to my wife, for fear the shock might be too great for her. By now the train was due to arrive shortly in Liverpool. He asked her if she had any news of me.

"I had a letter from a woman on the pilgrimage," she answered, "and it upset me very much. It said that Jack was dying and would never leave Lourdes alive. But just today I had a telegram from himself saying that he is feeling better."

She thought that I was only back to my ordinary state of bad health, having got over the danger I seemed to be in, while in Lourdes.

"The train will be in shortly, Mrs Traynor," said Fr Dawber, "and I think it would be nice to go down to meet it. But suppose you find Jack improved quite a bit, will you promise me that you won't get upset?"

"To be sure, Father," she answered, "I'll promise. And I'll be glad if I see him improved."

"Suppose you see him walking, Mrs Traynor?"

"Father, I'm afraid I'll never see Jack walk. But anyhow you can rely on me."

My wife went down to the station with her friend, Mrs Reitdyk. It seemed as if all Liverpool had gathered there. The people had seen the news of the miracle in the evening papers and had come down to see me. There were extra police on duty to handle the crowd, while railway officials stood at the entrance to the platform to keep the people from rushing the train.

With difficulty my wife and her friend reached the platform gate, where she told the official that she was Mrs Traynor and asked to be allowed through.

"Well," replied the man, "all I can say is that Mr Traynor must be a Mohammedan, because there are seventy or eighty Mrs Traynors on the platform already!"

Anyhow he let them through, and they waited on the platform. Meanwhile the railway company had decided that the only safe thing was to stop the train outside the station. They did this, and then the Archbishop walked towards the crowd, now a huge one, and addressed it. He asked the people to be orderly, and asked them to promise that if they just saw Traynor walk down the platform, they would be satisfied and would disperse. They assured him that they would.

But when I did appear on the platform, there was a stampede. The police had to draw their batons to force a passage for my wife and myself to a taxi. My brother got a blow on the side of the head before he could fight his way into the taxi with me.

We drove home, and I cannot describe the joy of my wife and children.

Permanent Cure

I am in the coal and haulage business now. I have four lorries or trucks and about a dozen men working for me. I work with them. I lift sacks of coal weighing around 200 pounds with the best of them and I can do any other work that an able-bodied man can do. But officially I am still classified as 100 per cent disabled and permanently incapacitated!

I never accepted a penny from anybody at the time of my cure or after it. I came back from Lourdes penniless, except for my war pension. I have never permitted any money to come to my family in connection with my cure or the publicity that has followed it. Nevertheless, Our Lady has improved my temporal affairs, too, and, thanks be to God and to Her, I am now comfortably situated, and my children are all well provided for. Three of them have been born since my cure, one a girl whom I have named Bernadette.

The two non-Catholic girls who looked after me when I came to Lourdes joined the Church as the result of my cure. Their family at home in Liverpool followed their example, and so did the Anglican minister of the church they had been attending. I know of another parson who would like to follow suit, only that he is a married man with a family. A large number of conversions in Liverpool have resulted from the miracle.

I go to Lourdes now every year and work as a brancardier there. I have gone twice and three times in one season.

Final Medical Report

On 7th July 1926, Traynor was examined again at Lourdes by Dr Vallet, president of the Medical Bureau, together with five other doctors, Drs Azurdia, Finn and Marley of Liverpool, who had examined him before and after his cure in 1923, Dr Harrington of Preston and Dr Moorkens of Antwerp. They found no trace of epilepsy or paralysis. His right arm was completely free from atrophy. The pectoral and shoulder muscles were fully restored. His wrist worked normally and he could use his right hand. As often happens in Lourdes cures, he had a souvenir of the injuries from which he had been miraculously liberated. The right hand does not hang quite normally; it is slightly en griffe. The right forearm is barely 1.55 cm. less thick than the left. The only trace of the hole in his skull was the slight depression that could be felt in the bone.

The official report, issued by the Medical Bureau at Lourdes on 2nd October, 1926, declared that "this extraordinary cure is absolutely beyond and above the powers of nature."

The most striking part of this multiple miracle is probably the instantaneous cure of the right arm. The nerves had been severed for eight years. Four surgical operations had revealed that they were truly severed and had failed to reunite them. More than mere suture would be necessary before the arm could feel and move again; the shrunken nerves would need to go through a long process of regeneration. A feat that expert surgery had failed four times to do and a process that requires months of gradual restoration were achieved instantaneously as the Blessed Sacrament was raised over John Traynor.

Another group of experts testified – though unconsciously – to the miracle. These were doctors and officials of the War Pensions Ministry. These gentlemen, after years of examination, treatment and inspection, certified that John Traynor was incurable, and they showed the strength of their conviction by awarding him full disability pension for life. They have never revoked that decision.

Epilogue

As I was about to publish this account, news has come that John Traynor died on the eve of the feast of the Immaculate Conception, 1943. The cause of his death was hernia, in no way related to the illness and wounds of which he was cured in Lourdes. For more than twenty years he lived a vigorous life, every moment of which he owed to the miracle of July 1923. For more than twenty years he was a standing, stalwart testimony to the power of Almighty God and the efficacy of the intercession of Mary Immaculate. In his rugged person he presented a tangible argument with which unbelief could not wrestle without being overthrown. For some this miracle has brought the surrender which is a gain and a victory. Others – it has happened from the beginning and will happen to the end – have taken flight from the facts, in one director or another.

Miracles such as the cure of John Traynor are, of course, rare, while they are real. They point the way not to a wide-open exit from all physical suffering but rather to the spiritual recoveries and triumphs that are certain to come from unhesitating faith and a childlike approach to Jesus Christ, through Mary, His Mother and ours.

From The Grotto

Bishop Crispian Hollis

Of all the popular images of Lourdes, this is the scene that is the most familiar to people, of whatever faith and none. Here we are, crowds of people, gathered at the Grotto in celebration and in prayer. This is the place which makes Lourdes special and different from any other place of pilgrimage in the World. We, who come, are drawn here and we keep coming back again and again.

Our first reading this morning spoke of the new Jerusalem, the place where God is to be found among his people. Lourdes is just such a place; it is a Holy place because God is here and He is at home with His people.

In spite of all the noise and bustle and constant movement of people, this is a Holy place because you can find a stillness here, and it's a stillness that betokens God's presence. Here, it's possible to hear and to tune into the still, small voice, the gentle breeze which tells us that we're in the presence of the Lord.

This is a Holy place because of what happened here all those years ago, because of the encounter that took place between Mary, the Mother and extraordinary messenger of God, and Bernadette, the poor one who was called by God to be the voice of many.

This place is Holy because it's where, as Bishop Mervyn so beautifully put it when he preached at our opening Mass, we come as the shepherds came to Bethlehem to tell Mary of the wonderful things God has been doing in our lives; here we can share with her, who is our Mother, the joys, the sadness, the

71

challenges, the successes and the failures of our lives.

This is a Holy place because you and I – and literally millions of others – have come here to pray and to catch a glimpse of the "new heavens and the new earth" that the Lord promises us and which is revealed in all the love and kindness that surrounds us.

But it's very important to acknowledge that we don't just bring Holy things here; we don't just bring a sanitised sort of life. We bring our most heartfelt feelings and emotions – the rawness of our lives – the anger, the hurt, the suffering, the distress and disappointment. Here too we can raise our voices and shake our fists at God if we feel He has let us down. We can do all this and, somehow, it doesn't matter, because we're at home and this is the family where we can be our true selves. We're all equal here and there's no rank or privilege. Despite the appearances, there's no hierarchy here that has any real significance. We come together as family and as children in the family of God.

And Mary? Well, she listens and smiles and ponders over everything that we have to say. She comforts and encourages us and she prays with us and shares our half – hesitant and fumbling prayer of conversion and healing.

This is her place and all are welcome into her home. It's a place for sinners and for those who want to be saints. It is, therefore, a place for miracles, for forgiveness, for renewal and for conversion. As often as that miracle of conversion takes place, then the seeds are sown for the "new heavens and the new earth".

But how can any of this take place? And how can it happen for me? Mary asked the angel the same question, though with less reason than us: "How can this be ?" She gives us the answer here that she heard from the angel. "Trust Him and you'll find that nothing is impossible for God – let what He says be done to you." This is the Mother's answer to our fears and doubts. The only thing that she insists on is that we don't come here and try to tell God what to do. When we have spoken, however hesitantly, and offered our prayers, then we must listen and we will be graced to do and to be what God wants of us.

This means that this is a place where we can pray huge, mad and extravagant prayers. We let go of ourselves here – the defences and facades crumble away and our prayers are able to go to the very heart of our longings. We are emptied and we become poor – without human privilege or distinction. This is how we pray prayers which leave us identified with and indistinguishable from the poorest of the poor. Our cries, which are so much ours, become the cry of the poor for the world which longs to experience solidarity and to be ruled by love and compassion.

Here also, we pray for the tragic and seemingly hopeless human horrors of our time – for Bosnia, for Somalia and for all those other situations which seem so desperate and fraught with evil and suffering.

We are able to pray with hope and confidence because here, before our eyes, we catch a glimpse of what is possible – "the new heavens and the new earth". We glimpse the renewed face of the earth because here the human family recognises and welcomes God. We can see the tears being wiped away; we see the end of death and mourning.

We see God among His people and ourselves alongside Him, playing our part in the transforming of the world. As often as this happens, and as often as we allow it to happen to us, then yet another miracle takes place and this holy place bears witness to the healing power of God.

The Way of the Cross
Fr Leudenger

His tormentors did everything to ridicule Him. They dressed Him in purple but it was for the purpose of deriding Him and making Him an object of scorn. They deprived Him of all His clothes, but it was in order to take away His inner grace, His richness and His being. They had made Him an object of mockery from whom they turned away in disgust. They killed His message, determined that its echo would be wiped off the face of the earth. Who would listen to a man on a cross?

Up to his death, He was excluded from society. It was outside the walls of Jerusalem that He was put to death. The walls of the town stood between Him and the city. He was marginalized like so many rejected human beings; ignored so that their misery and suffering remain unseen. He was relegated to the bottom of the pile reserved for the extreme poor; those who had nothing left to give: in exchange for His condemned state, only His innocence and His justice remained. As the thief on the Cross said: "We must pay for what we have done, but He was going to shed His blood in order to bring life to the love of God."

Jesus walked up the narrow and crowded streets which lead to Calvary. His strength was declining after the outrages that He had suffered. He buckled under the weight of the Cross and another man had to be called to help Him. He left behind all those moments of human happiness and joyous hope, but also His distraught disciples, His worried Mother, the crowds that had followed Him as following a shepherd, the Holy town whose people He was born amongst. It was Satan's hour, the hour when the world rejected light, the hour when sin burst out in all its murderous strength. Jesus was dying suffocated by the sin of the world. The ascendancy of evil needed Him. The Son of God found himself submitting to the power of evil, and the impossibility of escaping from it.

In this instance Jesus took the poor under His wing: those dragged through the mud and rejected from society, without sin, and only because of a malformed body of spirit, a bad family, an unhealthy environment or the colour of their skin. Even the worst killer, when he is placed beyond the crowd, booed at and lynched, takes on the face of Jesus on the Cross. Jesus and the victim become one.

Jesus doesn't only take extreme cases under His wing. No matter what our sins and our weaknesses, no matter what part we play in the test that awaits us, when we suffer, Jesus is with us, agonizing on the cross for us. When we are delivered from the blows of life by death or illness, through the fault of those close to us or that of society; when we find ourselves subjugated to economic laws which lead us to unemployment, reducing us to the object state, seducing us by all the means at their disposal, dehumanising us, we are victims.

Jesus crucified is therefore the only way of making sense of our lives. Certainly we reach Him through our thoughts, but we become like Him when we submit ourselves to the test. Jesus has us under His wing. We walk our way of the Cross. Sometimes like Him, we have the impression that our life is in shreds. We find ourselves vulnerable and deprived, abandoning all our friends and possessions. Who amongst us hasn't known the solitude of Gethsemane? Who doesn't feel condemned by the judgements, betrayals and abandonment of those close to us? Who amongst us doesn't know the bitter taste of despair, doubt or depression...? Just like Simon of Cyrene, we must carry the burden of others. Like Mary, we cry over so much suffering, for so many innocent victims. It's difficult to let go: to have faith. It is, nevertheless, in our extreme poverty when all seems lost, that life can burst out in us as it burst out in Jesus when he was condemned to death. A strange victory for life over sin and death.

This victory harbours no taste of vengeance or revenge. This victory is not the promise of human success to come. It is the birth of a more profound and stronger inner life, where we can find peace and joy. Mary and Bernadette understood this and guide us on our path following the pilgrims of Emmaus. Like them, we are invited to discover in shared pain our ray of light and the way in which we can construct our lives, perhaps during difficult times, but always in hope.

If it happens that one day we have a particularly difficult way of the Cross to climb, let us nourish ourselves from Him, who gives His life in the Eucharistic bread. Then, we shall perceive the light of our salvation at the end of our particular way. Our lives will be transformed by the way we face our trials. Brothers and Sisters, we travel the way of the Cross that Our Lord travelled. Each day, in our own lives, we walk a little further. Join Him so that we are a part of the light of the Passover.

A Place of Grace

Have you ever seen an ugly deformed person look beautiful? It is a contradiction in terms, but that is what happens in Lourdes. One of the most inspiring sights is to see a twisted body transformed into beauty, it is as if the soul of the pilgrim shines forth.

Every human being is indescribably beautiful because he or she is made in the image and likeness of God. Each one of us possesses that radiant exquisite beauty that becomes alive with the grace from God. In Lourdes, often described as a 'little bit of heaven upon earth', you glimpse a little of the splendour and beauty of the human soul, and it is most noticeable in the sick and handicapped pilgrims.

One of the most amazing events in Lourdes, is the Blessed Sacrament Procession. Our Lady, in one of her requests to Bernadette, asked if 'people would come here in procession'. It seemed an odd sort of request. The procession starts from the Grotto of Masabielle with a Bishop holding the Blessed Sacrament in a monstrance under a canopy held by brancardiers. The procession normally contains around 15,000 – 20,000 people. It leaves the Grotto area and starts on its journey. It is as if Our Lady is asking us to walk with Our Lord.

In the procession there are generally around 2,000-3,000 sick pilgrims in wheelchairs and stretchers. There are many banners from various parishes and diocese worldwide giving a huge effect of colour and splendour. The singing is magnificent from the choirs and from the pilgrims. However the nature of this procession is remarkable. You are in the presence of thousands of fellow Christians, with sick and handicapped pilgrims, Bishops, Priests, Religious, all walking, but in the midst of this great throng is Our Lord Jesus Christ.

Unquestionably he says to each pilgrim, "Walk with me – I am with you on this journey, and on your journey to eternity". One wishes that the procession would last forever.

If you should visit Lourdes you may find the answer to your doubts, worries and frustrations. Lourdes challenges the concepts of materialism, humanism, rationalism, fundamentalism and all the other isms that plague our society.

It is quite remarkable how you can find many moments of peace and tranquillity among thousands of chattering pilgrims. It is a great place of grace. Sanctifying grace seems to shower down from Heaven. It is a place of grace because there is such a huge concentration of people locked in prayer and penance. It is a place of grace because there is much suffering being offered to God for the conversion of sinners. It is a place of grace because the Mother of God came from Heaven and appeared to Bernadette. It is said, when speaking about Lourdes, "For unbelievers no explanation is possible, for believers no explanation is necessary". Yet even to those who would dismiss the apparitions as nonsense, they have to consider all the authenticated cures that have taken place, and are still taking place. They have to consider the incorruptibility of St Bernadette's body. They have to consider that the Catholic Church proclaimed the Dogma of the Immaculate Conception four years before the apparitions took place. The words "I am the Immaculate Conception" confirm the infallible teaching of the church and confirm original sin. In confirming original sin those words signify the fall of man, confirm her motherhood of Christ, and confirm the act of redemption of the human race.

If you visit Lourdes you will find Mary awaiting you, her arms extended towards you with a great smile of welcome.

The Apparitions

Bernadette was born on Sunday 7th January 1844 to Francois and Louise Soubirous. By 1856 the family was in desperate financial circumstances, unable to pay the rent they were made homeless, but a cousin, Andre Sajous, had pity on them and let the family move into the old Gaol room in Petit Fossés Street. The room measured around 16ft x 16ft. It had been abandoned by the police as being unhealthy.

The family, by this time, consisted of Toinette, aged ten, Jean-Marie, aged four, Justin who was born on 28th February 1855, and of course Bernadette who was twelve years old. The family lived in abject poverty in a dungeon, and on top of this Bernadette suffered from chronic Asthma. Their home was described by Andre Sajous in 1875 as follows: "The room was dark. In the back-yard was the privy which over-flowed and made the place smell. The Soubirous were destitute. Two poor beds, one on the right as you entered, the other on the same side near the fire place. They had one small trunk to put all their linen in. My wife lent them chemises. They were full of vermin. She often gave them a bit of bread made of millet. Yet the little ones never asked for anything. They would rather have starved."

Thus it was that the Mother of God chose to appear to this poverty stricken child. But Bernadette discovered that there is a poverty worse than destitution, hunger, cold and social degradation, and this is the poverty of sin.

First apparition – 11th February 1858. I went to the Grotto with Toinette and Jeanne Abadie to gather firewood. They crossed the water of the River Gave, I started to take my stockings off, when I heard a sound like a gust of wind. The trees were quite still. I heard the same sound again – as I raised my head to look at the Grotto I saw a Lady dressed in white, wearing a white dress, a blue girdle and a yellow rose on each foot, the same colour as the chain of her rosary. The beads of the rosary were white.

The Lady made a sign for me to approach; but I was seized with fear and I did not dare; thinking that I was faced with an illusion, I rubbed my eyes, but in vain; I looked again, and I could still see the same Lady.

Then I put my hand into my pocket, and took out my rosary. I wanted to make the sign of the Cross, but in vain. I could not raise my hand to my forehead, it kept on dropping. Then a violent impression took hold of me more strongly, but I did not go.

The Lady took the rosary that she held in her hands and she made the sign of the cross. Then I commenced not to be afraid.

I took my rosary again. I was able to make the sign of the Cross; from that moment I felt perfectly undisturbed in mind. I knelt down and said my rosary, seeing this Lady always before my eyes. The vision slipped the beads of her rosary between her fingers, but she did not move her lips.

When I had said my rosary the Lady made a sign for me to approach, but I did not dare. I stayed in the same place. Then, all of a sudden, she disappeared.

Our Lady appeared eighteen times to St Bernadette, and spoke to her five times. During the third Apparition, Our Lady asked Bernadette to come to the Grotto.

"Would you do me the favour of coming here for fourteen days." She also said to Bernadette "I do not promise to make you happy in this world, but in the next."

In the eighth Apparition Our Lady says to Bernadette "Do penance for sinners."

During the ninth Apparition Our Lady called for penance, and repeats the request three times. She asks Bernadette to eat the grass, as an act of penance. She also asks Bernadette to wash in the stream, pointing to a spot below the Grotto. Bernadette dug the ground with her fingers, a trickle of water appeared, soon to turn into a torrent.

In the tenth Apparition Our Lady says to Bernadette "I wish people to come here in procession and a Chapel to be built".

And the very last words spoken to Bernadette in the sixteenth Apparition. When asked three times to reveal who she was, the Lady joined her hands, raised her eyes to Heaven and said, "I am the Immaculate Conception".

Bernadette joined the Congregation of the Sisters of Charity as a Postulant in 1866. In 1867 she made her religious profession, taking the vows of poverty, chastity, obedience and charity. She remained at the Convent of St Gildard at Nevers until her death on the 16th April 1879, aged 35.

Bernadette Incorrupt

On Wednesday 16th April 1879 at 3 pm Sister Marie Bernard left this life. An Episcopal committee was set up to examine Bernadette's reputation for saintliness, virtue and miracles surrounding the visions at Lourdes. After 30 years the commission had completed it's work. The next step in the process of canonization was the first "identification of the body" as it is called, which implies identification in accordance with civil and canon law, and verification of the state of the corpse.

On Wednesday 22nd September 1909 the body of Bernadette was exhumed. Monsignor Gauthey, Bishop of Nevers, and the Church tribunal, entered the main chapel of the convent at 8.30 am. A table had been placed at the entrance to the sanctuary. On it were the Holy Gospels. One by one, the three witnesses (Abbe Perreau, the Mother Superior of the order, Marie Josephine Forestier, and her deputy) the doctors (Doctors Jourdan and David), the stonemasons, Gavillon and Boue, and the carpenters, Cognet and Mary, swore an oath to tell the truth. The party then moved on to the chapel of St Joseph. The local mayor and the deputy mayor insisted on carrying out the legal formalities in person. Once the stone had been lifted from the vault the coffin was immediately visible. It was carried to the room prepared for it and placed on two trestles covered with a cloth. On one side was a table covered with a white cloth. The body – or, if applicable, the bones – of Bernadette were to be placed on this table. The wooden coffin was unscrewed and the lead coffin cut open. The assembled group looked at the interior of the coffin in amazement. The Sisters fell to their knees. The Bishop of Nevers joined his hands in a prayer of joyous thanksgiving. The stonemasons, the carpenters, stood with their eyes bulging and mouths hanging open. The doctors shook their heads in amazement, for what each one present saw was the body of Bernadette in a state of perfect preservation.

There was not the slightest trace of an unpleasant smell. The Sisters who had buried her thirty years earlier noted only that her hands had fallen slightly to the left. But the words of the surgeon and the doctor, who were under oath, speak for themselves:

"The coffin was opened in the presence of the Bishop of Nevers, the mayor of the town, his principal deputy, several canons and ourselves. We noticed no smell. The body was clothed in the habit of Bernadette's order. The habit was damp. Only the face, hands and forearms were uncovered.

The head was tilted to the left. The face was matt white. The skin clung to the muscles and the muscles adhered to the bones. The sockets of the eyes were covered by the eyelids. The brows were flat on the skin and stuck to the arches above the eyes. The lashes of the right eyelid were stuck to the skin. The nose was dilated and shrunken. The mouth was open slightly and it could be seen that the teeth were still in place. The hands, which were crossed on her breast, were perfectly preserved, as were the nails. The hands still held a rusting rosary. The veins on the forearms stood out.

Like the hands, the feet were wizened and the

toenails were still intact (one of them was torn off when the corpse was washed). When the habits had been removed and the veil lifted from the head, the whole of the shrivelled body could be seen, rigid and taut in every limb.

It was found that the hair, which had been cut short, was stuck to the head and still attached to the skull – that the ears were in a state of perfect preservation – that the left-hand side of the body was slightly higher than the right from the hip up.

The stomach had caved in and was taut like the rest of the body. It sounded like cardboard when struck.

The left knee was not as large as the right. The ribs protruded as did the muscles in the limbs.

So rigid was the body that it could be rolled over and back for washing.

The lower parts of the body had turned slightly black. This seems to have been the result of the carbon of which quite large quantities were found in the coffin.

In the witness of which we have duly drawn up this present statement in which all is truthfully recorded.

22 Nevers, September, 1909
Drs Ch. David, A. Jourdan"

The nuns washed the body and replaced it in a new coffin lined with zinc and padded with white silk. In the few hours in which it had been exposed to the air the body had started turning black. The double coffin was closed, soldered, screwed down and sealed with seven seals.

The labourers once again bore Bernadette's body

into the vault. It was 5.30 pm by the time everything had been completed.

The fact that Bernadette's body was perfectly preserved is not necessarily miraculous. It is well known that corpses decompose less in certain kinds of soil and gradually mummify. It should be noted, however, that in the case of Bernadette this mummified state is quite astounding. Her illnesses and the state of her body when she died, the humidity in the vault in the chapel of St Joseph (the habit was damp, the rosary rusty and the crucifix had turned green) would all seem to be conducive to disintegration of the flesh. But this is not a "miracle" in the strictest sense of the word.

Second "Identification of the Body": 3rd April 1919

On 13th August 1913, Pope Pius X, in consequence of a decision of the Congregation of Rites, authorised the introduction of the cause of beatification and canonization of Bernadette Soubirous and signed the decree of venerability. War broke out and it was impossible to take up the case again immediately. This was not done until 1918, at which time Monsignor Chatelus was bishop of Nevers.

This made another identification of the body of the venerable Bernadette necessary. Dr Talon and Dr Comte were asked to undertake the examination. It took place on 3rd April 1919, in the presence of the Bishop of Nevers, the police commissioner, representatives of the municipalities and members of the church tribunal.

Everything was just the same as at the time of the first exhumation. Oaths were sworn, the vault was opened, the body transferred to a new coffin and re-buried, all in accordance with canon and civil law. After the doctors had examined the body, they were each shut up alone in separate rooms to write their personal reports without being able to consult each other.

The two reports coincide perfectly with each other and also with Doctor Jourdan and Doctor David's report of 1909. There is one new element as regards the state of the body. This is the existence of "patches of mildew and a layer of salt which seems to be calcium salt," and which were probably the result of the body having been washed the first time it was exhumed. We will quote only the first few lines of Dr. Comte's report: "When the coffin was opened the body appeared to be absolutely intact and odour-less." (Dr Talon was more specific: "There was no smell of putrefaction and none of those present expe-rienced any discomfort.") The body is practically mummified, covered with patches of mildew and quite a notable layer of salts which appear to be calcium salts. The skeleton is complete, and it was possible to carry the body to a table without any trouble. Some of the veins are still visible."

At 5 pm that evening the body was reburied in the Chapel of St Joseph in the presence of the Bishop, Mother Forestier and the police commissioner.

Third "Identification of the Body" and Removal of Relics: 18th April 1925

On 18th November 1923, the Pope pronounced the authenticity of Bernadette's virtues and the path to beatification was open.

A third and final identification of the body was

required for the proclamation of beatification. The relics, which were to go to Rome, Lourdes, or houses of the Order, were to be taken during this exhumation.

Doctor Talon and Doctor Comte were once again asked to examine the body and Dr Comte, who was a surgeon was to remove the relics.

The ceremony took place on 18th April 1925, forty-six years and two days after Bernadette's death. The ceremony was private as is required by canon law when beatification has not yet been pronounced. Present were the nuns from the community, the Bishop, the vicars-general, the church tribunal, two "instrumental" witnesses, the two doctors, Mabille, the commissioner of police, and Leon Bruneton, representing the municipal authorities.

At 8.30 am in the chapel of the convent the two doctors whose task it was to examine the body for the official identification and the masons and carpenters who were to open the vault and take out the coffin swore the usual oaths on the gospels.

"I solemnly swear and promise faithfully to accomplish the task with which I have been entrusted," declared the doctors, "and to tell the truth in the replies I make to questions put to me and in my written statements on the examination of the body of the Venerable Servant of God, Sister Marie-Bernard Soubirous, and on the removal of the relics. This I solemnly promise and swear. So help me God and the Holy Gospels." And each of the labourers took an oath: "With my hand on God's gospels I solemnly swear and promise faithfully to accomplish the task with which I have been entrusted. So help me God and the Holy Gospels."

The body was in a perfect state of preservation.

Bernadette was beatified by Pope Pius XI on 14th

June 1925, and canonised by the same Pope on 8th December, the feast of the Immaculate conception 1933. The holy Catholic Church proclaimed to the world that Bernadette is in heaven. Bernadette's body remains incorrupt and you can see it in a crystal casket near the high altar at the Chapel of St Gildard at Nevers in France. This preservation of Bernadette's body is a fact. The physical evidence is available, and the incorruptibility has never been challenged. This continuing incorruptibility of the body is a continuing extraordinary type of "miracle"; it is a sign or a seal from Heaven on the truths of her visions and of her place among the saints.

This preservation of Bernadette's body is a deliberate act of God designed to awaken our souls and help us to discover the true destiny that awaits each of us when we leave this mortal life.

LOURDES: CITY OF THE SICK

Catherine T. Watling

Lourdes: city of the sick, is the moving story of a shepherd, Con Brannigan, who began his days in the bleak Cumbrian fells. He became afflicted with multiple sclerosis, his illness was totally unacceptable to his sons and wife. Con was given the opportunity to join the local pilgrimage to Lourdes. They wanted a miracle for him, he too wanted one. Although no visible signs of physical change occurred, there was a remarkable transformation in his mental outlook and attitude. This was Con's miracle at Lourdes.

The author offers us a picturesque description of Lourdes, its impelling force and its magnetic effect... to keep going there year after year. The book itself makes very pleasurable reading of a moving story.

Con's story is a beautiful one – it's real, it has happened! – and beautifully written too. The message is obvious and clear: it shows that a miracle is not the extraordinary event restoring lost limbs but... something we can all 'see' repeated in our lives.

CATHERINE T. WATLING was born in Northern Ireland. She left her hometown to embark on a nursing career. She was an assessor on the Examining Board for the General Nursing Council. Now retired, she lives with her husband in the north west of England.

ISBN 085439 445 1   123 pp (+ 8 pp of illus.)